LOGISTICS 4.0
Embracing Technology in Supply Chain Transformation

CLIVE AKHALUMENYO

Copyright © 2024. Clive Akhalumenyo. All Rights Reserved
Logistics 4.0

ISBN: 978-9-9471-2171-9

No part of this book may be reproduced or transmitted in any form—electronic, mechanical, photocopying, recording, or any information storage and retrieval system—without prior written permission from the copyright owner.

This material is intended solely for educational and informational purposes.

The author and publisher do not endorse commercial products or services linked to this book.

Globally Available

Published by:
Emphaloz Publishing House
publish@emphaloz.com

CONTENTS

FOREWORD V

INTRODUCTION VII

CHAPTER ONE
Introduction To Logistics 4.0   1

CHAPTER TWO
The Evolution of Supply Chain Technology   7

CHAPTER THREE
Industry 4.0 and Its Impact on Logistics   15

CHAPTER FOUR
The Role of AI and Machine Learning in Supply Chains   23

CHAPTER FIVE
Smart Warehousing and Automation   30

CHAPTER SIX
Blockchain and Supply Chain Transparency.   40

CHAPTER SEVEN
The Role of Data Analytics in Decision-Making   53

CHAPTER EIGHT
Sustainable Supply Chains with Technology   64

CHAPTER NINE
Challenges and Risks in Adopting Logistics 4.0   76

CHAPTER TEN
The Future of Supply Chain Management   89

APPENDIX   102
GLOSSARY OF ACRONYMS   109
ABOUT THE AUTHOR   110

FOREWORD

The world of logistics is undergoing a dramatic shift. As we stand on the brink of a technological revolution, supply chains, which have long been the backbone of global commerce, are evolving at a pace we've never seen before. What once required manual processes and extensive human intervention is now being transformed by technologies like artificial intelligence, automation, and blockchain. This transformation—Logistics 4.0—offers unparalleled opportunities to redefine how we move goods, manage resources, and deliver value. In my years working in the supply chain industry, I have witnessed first-hand the incredible advances that have led us to this moment. We are at a pivotal point where technology is no longer just a tool; it is becoming the cornerstone of supply chain strategy, driving innovation and unlocking new levels of efficiency. This book is not just a guide to understanding the components of Logistics 4.0—it is a blueprint for embracing the future. Whether you are a logistics professional looking to adapt to new realities, an industry leader seeking ways to stay competitive, or simply someone curious about the technologies reshaping global commerce, this book offers insights that will prepare you for what lies ahead. Through a combination of practical examples, case studies, and expert analysis, Logistics 4.0: Embracing Technology in Supply Chain Transformation lays out the roadmap for building smarter, more agile, and sustainable supply chains. It dives into the key technologies reshaping our industry and explores how businesses can leverage them to remain at the forefront of innovation.

I invite you to start this journey with an open mind and a readiness to embrace the possibilities of what the future holds. The revolution in logistics is here, and the time to act is now.

Enjoy the read and let the transformation begin!

INTRODUCTION

The logistics and supply chain industry is a vital cog in the machinery of global trade. From manufacturing and warehousing to transportation and last-mile delivery, logistics plays a crucial role in ensuring that goods flow seamlessly across borders, industries, and economies. Yet, as essential as this function is, the supply chain landscape is undergoing profound changes—driven by technology, shifting consumer demands, and the need for greater agility and sustainability. This book, **"Logistics 4.0: Embracing Technology in Supply Chain Transformation,"** is about understanding and navigating this evolving landscape. At its core, Logistics 4.0 represents the next wave of supply chain innovation, where traditional processes are enhanced or even replaced by digital technologies. These advancements are not just upgrades, they are a complete overhaul of how goods are sourced, produced, and delivered. In recent years, technological disruption has touched nearly every sector, and logistics is no exception. Concepts that once seemed futuristic—like automated warehouses, AI-driven forecasting, and blockchain-based transparency—are quickly becoming the standard. Companies that fail to adapt will find themselves lagging behind, while those that embrace these technologies will unlock new efficiencies, better customer experiences, and more sustainable practices.

But what exactly is Logistics 4.0, and why does it matter so much?

This introduction will explore the key drivers behind Logistics 4.0 and the role that digital transformation plays in reshaping the industry. It will delve into the opportunities that this new wave of technology offers and highlight the risks and challenges companies face as they make this transition. By the end, you will have a clear understanding of why embracing Logistics 4.0 is not just a strategic choice but an imperative for staying competitive in today's fast-paced world.

The Rise of Digital Supply Chains

The journey to Logistics 4.0 begins with the rise of digital supply chains. Unlike traditional models, where logistics relied heavily on manual processes, digital supply chains are powered by data, automation, and smart systems. Technologies such as the Internet of Things (IoT), artificial intelligence (AI), and cloud computing have transformed how supply chains operate, enabling companies to respond faster to changes in demand, reduce costs, and optimize every aspect of their operations. In this new era, supply chains are becoming smarter, more interconnected, and more transparent. Companies can track goods in real time, predict potential disruptions, and make data-driven decisions that improve efficiency and sustainability.

Why Logistics 4.0 Matters

The shift to Logistics 4.0 is not merely a technological upgrade, it's a response to the increasing complexity of global supply chains. Today, businesses face more challenges than ever before, rising customer expectations, regulatory pressures, sustainability demands, and the need for speed and accuracy in delivering products. In such an environment, traditional supply chain management simply won't cut it. Logistics 4.0 addresses these challenges by offering smarter, more adaptive solutions. Through automation, data analytics, and digital integration, companies can improve their responsiveness to market changes, reduce waste, and better manage risks. The transformation is already underway, and those who adopt it early will have a significant advantage.

What This Book Covers

Throughout this book, we will explore the key technologies driving Logistics 4.0, from AI and robotics to blockchain and IoT. We'll look at real-world examples of companies that have successfully implemented these technologies and examine the impact on their operations. We will also discuss the challenges businesses face during this transition, including the skills gap, cybersecurity concerns, and integration hurdles. Each chapter will guide you through a different aspect of Logistics 4.0, providing insights, strategies, and actionable steps that can be applied to your own supply chain processes. This book is designed for logistics professionals, business leaders, and anyone looking to understand the future of supply chain management. Whether you are starting your journey toward digital transformation or are already on the path, "Logistics 4.0: Embracing Technology in Supply Chain Transformation" will serve as your guide to unlocking the potential of modern logistics.

Welcome to the future of logistics, where technology is the key to unlocking new possibilities. Let's dive in.

"The best way to predict the future is to create it."
– Peter Drucker

"In the midst of every crisis, lies a great opportunity."
– Albert Einstein

"It is not the strongest of the species that survive, nor the most intelligent, but the one most responsive to change."
– Charles Darwin

"Technology is best when it brings people together."
– Matt Mullenweg

"Innovation distinguishes between a leader and a follower."
– Steve Jobs

CHAPTER ONE
Introduction To Logistics 4.0

Supply chains have always been the unseen force driving global commerce. From raw materials sourced from distant regions to the delivery of finished goods to consumers, the journey a product takes through the supply chain is long and complex. However, the processes that once relied on manual coordination, human decision-making, and basic tracking systems are now on the brink of transformation. This is where Logistics 4.0 comes into play. In the early days of supply chain management, processes were predominantly manual. Companies relied heavily on paperwork, telephone calls, and personal relationships to keep goods flowing.

Over time, with the advent of computer systems and enterprise resource planning (ERP) software, supply chains became more organized, though they still required significant human intervention. However, today's world demands far more. Companies now need supply chains that are faster, smarter, and more agile than ever before. Logistics 4.0 is the response to this demand. It leverages the power of digitalization, automation, and data analytics to create supply chains that can respond to changes in real time. This new approach is not just about efficiency, it's about fundamentally changing how logistics operations are managed, monitored, and optimized.

What is Logistics 4.0?

Logistics 4.0 refers to the integration of advanced technologies, such as the Internet of Things (IoT), artificial intelligence (AI), cloud computing, blockchain, and robotics, into supply chain operations. It is closely tied to the broader concept of Industry 4.0, which refers to the fourth industrial revolution characterized by smart factories and automation. In Logistics 4.0, data becomes the cornerstone of decision-making. Sensors and devices capture data at every stage of the supply chain, from production lines to warehouses to distribution centers. This data is then analyzed in real time, providing companies with insights that allow them to optimize everything from inventory management to transportation routes. For example, instead of waiting for a shipment to arrive and manually updating records, a smart supply chain using IoT-enabled devices can track shipments in real time, predict arrival times, and alert managers to any delays. Similarly, AI algorithms can forecast demand patterns, enabling businesses to adjust inventory levels automatically, reducing waste and increasing efficiency.

Key Drivers Behind Logistics 4.0

Several factors have contributed to the rise of Logistics 4.0:

Consumer Expectations: In today's world, consumers expect faster deliveries, real-time tracking, and personalized services. E-commerce giants like Amazon have set a new standard, pushing businesses to rethink how they manage their supply chains.

Globalization: As supply chains become more global and complex, the need for advanced technologies to manage multiple touchpoints across borders has become critical. Logistics 4.0 helps businesses handle these complexities with greater accuracy and speed.

Technological Advancements: The rapid development of technologies like AI, blockchain, and IoT has made it easier for companies to automate processes and make data-driven decisions.

Sustainability: The pressure to create more sustainable and environmentally friendly supply chains has pushed companies to adopt new technologies that minimize waste, reduce carbon footprints, and enhance transparency.

One of the key benefits of Logistics 4.0 is the agility it offers to businesses. In a world where disruptions are increasingly common, whether it's a natural disaster, a pandemic, or geopolitical tensions—supply chains must be able to adapt quickly to changing conditions. Traditional supply chains, with their reliance on linear processes and manual interventions, are often slow to react to disruptions. In contrast, a Logistics 4.0-enabled supply chain can instantly identify bottlenecks, reroute shipments, and adjust production schedules based on real-time data. This agility allows companies to stay ahead of potential problems and continue delivering value to customers, even in the face of unforeseen challenges.

A New Era of Collaboration

Logistics 4.0 also fosters a new level of collaboration within the supply chain ecosystem. With technologies like blockchain, companies can create shared, immutable records of transactions and goods movements, ensuring transparency and trust among all parties. Suppliers, manufacturers, distributors, and retailers can all access the same real-time data, improving coordination and reducing the risk of errors or delays. This collaborative approach extends to customers as well. With real-time visibility in the status of orders, customers feel more connected to the process, which enhances their overall experience and satisfaction.

A Competitive Advantage

In the race to stay competitive, adopting Logistics 4.0 can provide businesses with a significant edge. Companies that leverage advanced technologies to optimize their supply chains are better positioned to meet customer demands, reduce costs, and minimize risks. They can also differentiate themselves in the marketplace by offering faster delivery times, greater transparency, and a more personalized customer experience. The shift to Logistics 4.0

is not just about survivalists thriving in a new era of supply chain management. Businesses that embrace this transformation will be better equipped to navigate the complexities of today's global economy, while those that resist may find themselves struggling to keep up. As we continue through this book, we will dive deeper into the specific technologies that drive Logistics 4.0, explore real-world examples of its implementation, and examine the potential challenges businesses face as they transition to this new model. From AI and robotics to blockchain and smart warehouses, each chapter will provide you with a comprehensive understanding of how Logistics 4.0 is shaping the future of supply chain management.

Logistics 4.0 is more than just a trend in the future of global commerce. Welcome to the journey.

CHAPTER TWO
The Evolution of Supply Chain Technology

The supply chain, as we know it today, is the result of centuries of evolution, shaped by the changing demands of global trade, industrial revolutions, and advancements in transportation. While the principles of moving goods from point A to point B have remained the same, the methods and technologies we use to achieve this have transformed dramatically. This chapter explores how supply chain management has evolved, from its earliest stages to the sophisticated, tech-driven systems of Logistics 4.0.

Early Supply Chains: The Foundations of Commerce

In ancient times, supply chains were simple and localized. Early civilizations engaged in trade by transporting goods via ships, carts, and on foot. These supply chains were limited by geography, weather, and the availability of resources. Markets were primarily regional, and logistics involved basic tasks like bartering, storage, and simple inventory management. As societies grew, so did the complexity of supply chains. The advent of currency, standard units of measurement, and written records enabled larger-scale trade, extending the reach of supply chains beyond local markets. The Silk Road, for example, was one of the earliest examples of a long-distance supply chain, linking China with Europe and facilitating the exchange of goods like silk, spices, and precious metals. However, even with this increased scope, supply chains remained rudimentary and labor-intensive, relying heavily on human coordination.

The Industrial Revolution: The Birth of Modern Logistics

The first significant leap in supply chain technology occurred during the Industrial Revolution in the 18th and 19th centuries. The introduction of steam engines, railroads, and mechanized production transformed not only manufacturing but also the way goods were transported and distributed. For the first time, businesses could produce goods on a scale, and supply chains began to stretch across continents. With the growth of industrial production came the need for more efficient logistics systems. Warehousing became more sophisticated, and transportation networks expanded rapidly. The steam engine, in particular, allowed for faster and more reliable shipping, reducing the time it took for goods to reach their destination. This era marked the beginning of the integration of technology into logistics, although processes still required significant manual oversight.

The Rise of Globalization and the Birth of Modern Supply Chains

The mid-20th century ushered in the era of globalization. Advancements in transportation, particularly the widespread use of shipping containers, airplanes, and highways, enabled companies to source materials and sell products across the globe. Supply chains became more interconnected, with goods flowing between multiple countries before reaching their final destination. This period also saw the rise of multinational corporations and complex manufacturing networks. Companies began outsourcing production to countries with lower labor costs, adding more layers to the supply chain. As a result, managing logistics became a more intricate process, requiring businesses to develop more robust systems for tracking, warehousing, and transportation. In response, the field of supply chain management began to formalize. Companies adopted new strategies like just-in-time (JIT) manufacturing, which sought to reduce waste and improve efficiency by aligning production schedules with consumer demand. The introduction of computers and early software systems in the 1970s and 1980s further improved the ability of companies to manage these increasingly complex supply chains.

The Digital Age: Entering the Era of Automation and Data

By the late 20th and early 21st centuries, the digital revolution began to change the face of supply chain management. The introduction of personal computers, the internet, and advanced software systems enabled businesses to automate many of their processes and make data-driven decisions. Enterprise resource planning (ERP) systems emerged, allowing companies to integrate all aspects of their supply chains into a single digital platform. For the first time, businesses could monitor their supply chains in real time, track inventory levels, predict demand, and manage their transportation networks with a level of precision that was previously unimaginable. Digital systems replaced paper-based processes, and companies could now share information across different departments and with external partners more efficiently. In this era, supply chains became increasingly global, with companies using digital tools to manage a vast network of suppliers, manufacturers, distributors, and customers across multiple continents. Technologies like RFID (Radio-Frequency Identification) tags and barcodes revolutionized inventory management, making it easier to track products at every stage of the supply chain.

The Role of Data and Analytics in the Modern Supply Chain

One of the most transformative elements of the digital age has been the role of data and analytics. As supply chains grew more complex, the ability to gather, analyze, and act on data became critical to maintaining efficiency and competitiveness. With the explosion of data generated by IoT devices, sensors, and digital transactions, supply chain managers now have access to more information than ever before. This data could be used to predict demand, optimize transportation routes, manage inventory levels, and even identify potential disruptions before they occur. For example, data analytics allowed companies to forecast seasonal demand spikes, ensuring they had enough inventory on hand to meet customer needs. It also enabled businesses to optimize their supply chain networks, reducing costs and improving delivery times.

The Road to Logistics 4.0

As we move further into the 21st century, the next stage of supply chain evolution is unfolding Logistics 4.0. This new era is driven by technologies that were once considered science fiction—artificial intelligence, machine learning, blockchain, and automation. These innovations are taking supply chain management to new heights, enabling companies to operate with greater speed, precision, and agility. Logistics 4.0 is not just about incremental improvements to existing processes. It represents a fundamental shift in how supply chains are managed and optimized. The focus is no longer just on efficiency but on creating smart, interconnected systems that can adapt to changing conditions in real-time. With the integration of AI and machine learning, companies can now make more informed decisions faster than ever. Automated systems handle everything from order processing to inventory management, reducing human error and increasing efficiency.

Blockchain technology ensures transparency and trust throughout the supply chain, while IoT devices provide real-time data on the location and condition of goods. The future of supply chain technology lies in the continued development and adoption of Logistics 4.0 principles. As more companies embrace digital transformation, supply chains will become even more connected, automated, and data driven. The integration of emerging technologies like drones, autonomous vehicles, and 3D printing will further revolutionize how goods are produced, transported, and delivered. While there are challenges to overcome—such as cybersecurity risks and the need for upskilling the workforce, the benefits of Logistics 4.0 far outweigh the risks. Companies that invest in these technologies will be better positioned to compete in a rapidly changing global market.

CHAPTER THREE
Industry 4.0 and Its Impact on Logistics

The world is currently undergoing a technological revolution that is fundamentally changing the way we produce, manage, and deliver goods. This revolution, known as Industry 4.0, brings together technologies like artificial intelligence (AI), machine learning, the Internet of Things (IoT), blockchain, and robotics to create smart factories, intelligent systems, and fully integrated supply chains. In this chapter, we will explore what Industry 4.0 is and its profound impact on the logistics sector.

What is Industry 4.0?

Industry 4.0 is often referred to as the Fourth Industrial Revolution. It represents the next phase in the digitization of manufacturing and production, where traditional industrial processes are enhanced by advanced digital technologies.

These technologies enable companies to operate with greater flexibility, accuracy, and efficiency. Unlike previous industrial revolutions, which focused on mechanization, mass production, and automation, Industry 4.0 centers on connectivity, data, and real-time insights. At its core, Industry 4.0 is about creating smart factories where machines, devices, and systems communicate with each other to optimize production and supply chain operations.

The key elements of Industry 4.0 include:

Internet of Things (IoT): The ability to connect machines, sensors, and devices to the internet, enabling them to share and process data in real time.

Artificial Intelligence (AI) and Machine Learning: Systems that can analyze large volumes of data to make decisions, predict outcomes, and optimize processes without human intervention.

Robotics and Automation: Advanced robots capable of performing complex tasks with precision and consistency.

Blockchain: A secure, transparent digital ledger that records transactions and tracks goods throughout the supply chain.

Cloud Computing: The use of remote servers to store, manage, and process data, allowing for easy access to information from anywhere in the world.

How Industry 4.0 is Transforming Logistics

The integration of Industry 4.0 technologies is reshaping the logistics landscape in unprecedented ways. Supply chains are no longer linear; they are becoming interconnected networks that can adapt to changes in real time. The benefits of this transformation are vast, ranging from improved efficiency to enhanced customer satisfaction. Below are some of the keyways Industry 4.0 is impacting logistics.

Real-Time Data and Visibility

One of the most significant impacts of Industry 4.0 on logistics is the ability to access and act on real-time data. With IoT devices embedded throughout the supply chain, companies can track the movement and condition of goods at every stage—from production to warehousing to final delivery. This real-time visibility allows businesses to respond quickly to disruptions or changes in demand. For example, if a shipment is delayed, supply chain managers can reroute goods to minimize the impact on customers. This level of agility was not possible in traditional supply chains, where delays often led to lengthy disruptions. In addition to improving responsiveness, real-time data also enhances transparency. Both businesses and customers can monitor the status of shipments, leading to greater trust and accountability.

Predictive Analytics and Demand Forecasting

Industry 4.0 technologies, such as AI and machine learning, have given rise to predictive analytics—a game-changing capability in logistics. By analyzing historical data and identifying patterns, AI-powered systems can predict future demand with remarkable accuracy. This allows companies to make more informed decisions about inventory levels, production schedules, and transportation routes. Predictive analytics can also help businesses identify potential bottlenecks before they occur, enabling them to take proactive measures to avoid disruptions. For example, retailers can use predictive analytics to anticipate seasonal demand spikes and adjust their inventory levels accordingly. Manufacturers can forecast equipment maintenance needs, reducing downtime and ensuring smooth operations.

Automation and Smart Warehousing

Automation has been a driving force in logistics for years, but with the advent of Industry 4.0, its impact has reached new heights. Smart warehouses, powered by robotics, IoT, and AI, are transforming how goods are stored, picked, packed, and shipped. In a smart warehouse, robots handle repetitive tasks like moving pallets, picking items from shelves, and packing boxes. IoT devices track the location of goods in real time, ensuring that inventory is always accounted for. Meanwhile, AI systems optimize warehouse layouts, ensuring that frequently ordered items are easily accessible. This automation leads to faster, more accurate fulfilment processes, reducing human error and minimizing the time it takes to get products to customers. It also frees up human workers to focus on more strategic tasks, such as improving customer service or optimizing supply chain strategies.

Blockchain and Supply Chain Transparency

Blockchain technology is revolutionizing supply chain transparency and traceability. In traditional supply chains, tracking the origin and movement of goods can be a cumbersome process, often requiring multiple intermediaries and manual paperwork. With blockchain, every transaction and movement of goods is recorded on a secure, decentralized ledger that cannot be altered. This ensures that all parties involved—suppliers, manufacturers, distributors, and customers—have access to a single, immutable source of truth. Blockchain is particularly valuable in industries where trust and authenticity are critical, such as pharmaceuticals and food. For example, blockchain can help trace the origin of a product, ensuring that it meets safety standards and has not been tampered with. This level of transparency builds trust with consumers and reduces the risk of fraud or counterfeiting.

Sustainability and Resource Optimization

Industry 4.0 is also driving sustainability efforts within logistics. Advanced technologies like AI, IoT, and robotics enable companies to optimize resource use, reducing waste and minimizing their environmental footprint. For example, AI-powered systems can analyze data to optimize transportation routes, reducing fuel consumption and emissions. Smart warehouses can minimize energy usage by automating lighting, heating, and cooling based on real-time demand. IoT devices can monitor the condition of perishable goods, reducing spoilage and ensuring that only high-quality products reach consumers.

Challenges of Implementing Industry 4.0 in Logistics

While the benefits of Industry 4.0 in logistics are clear, the road to implementation is not without challenges. Some of the key obstacles businesses face include:

Cost of Adoption: Implementing Industry 4.0 technologies can be expensive, particularly for small and medium-sized enterprises (SMEs). The cost of upgrading infrastructure, purchasing new equipment, and training employees can be a significant barrier to adoption.

Cybersecurity: As supply chains become more digitized and interconnected, they also become more vulnerable to cyberattacks. Ensuring the security of sensitive data and systems is a top priority for businesses adopting Industry 4.0 technologies.

Workforce Skills Gap: The shift to Industry 4.0 requires a workforce with new skills, particularly in areas like data analytics, AI, and robotics. Many businesses struggle to find workers with the necessary expertise to implement and manage these technologies.

The Future of Logistics in the Age of Industry 4.0

As Industry 4.0 technologies continue to evolve, their impact on logistics will only grow. In the future, we can expect to see even greater levels of automation, connectivity, and data-driven decision-making. Drones and autonomous vehicles may become a common sight in logistics operations, while AI systems will play an even larger role in managing supply chains end-to-end. Companies that embrace Industry 4.0 will be well-positioned to thrive in this new era. By adopting these technologies, businesses can create smarter, more efficient, and more resilient supply chains that can adapt to the demands of a rapidly changing global market.

CHAPTER FOUR
The Role of AI and Machine Learning in Supply Chains

The future of logistics and supply chain management is being shaped by the intelligent application of advanced technologies such as Artificial Intelligence (AI) and Machine Learning (ML). These powerful tools are transforming how businesses predict, plan, and execute operations across the supply chain, driving efficiency, accuracy, and responsiveness. AI and ML are not just enhancing existing processes, they are revolutionizing the supply chain, creating smarter, more agile systems capable of adapting to ever-changing market conditions. Artificial Intelligence refers to machines' ability to simulate human intelligence, learn from data, identify patterns, make decisions, and automate processes. Machine Learning, a subset of AI, focuses on developing algorithms that enable machines to improve their decision-making capabilities through experience and historical data analysis. In supply chains, AI and ML are applied to optimize a wide range of activities, from demand forecasting and inventory management to risk mitigation and automation.

One of the most transformative applications of AI in supply chains is demand forecasting. Traditionally, companies relied on historical data, consumer behavior trends, and market forecasts to estimate future demand. These methods were often prone to inaccuracies, leading to overstocking, stockouts, and missed opportunities. AI dramatically improves forecasting accuracy by analyzing vast amounts of data from various sources, including past sales, economic indicators, social trends, and even real-time consumer behavior. As machine learning algorithms continuously refine their predictions, businesses can dynamically adjust their strategies to better meet consumer demand. For example, AI systems can identify seasonal spikes in demand for certain products or detect emerging trends, enabling businesses to optimize stock levels and reduce waste.

In addition to demand forecasting, AI plays a crucial role in inventory management. Managing inventory levels effectively is a delicate balance—too much stock ties up capital and increases storage costs, while too little stock risks losing sales. AI-powered systems analyze data on past sales, supplier lead times, and real-time market conditions to dynamically adjust inventory levels. These systems ensure businesses maintain optimal stock levels, reducing both carrying costs and the risk of stockouts. With predictive capabilities, AI can forecast potential overstock or understock situations, giving companies the ability to make proactive adjustments.

Automation is another area where AI and machine learning are making a significant impact in supply chains, particularly in warehousing and distribution. Smart warehouses, powered by AI-driven robots and IoT devices, are streamlining operations by automating tasks such as picking, packing, and sorting items. These systems use AI to optimize warehouse layouts, ensuring that frequently ordered items are easily accessible and reducing the time it takes to fulfil orders. As a result, businesses experience faster, more accurate fulfilment processes, reducing human error and accelerating delivery times. Moreover, AI systems can manage transportation logistics, optimizing delivery routes based on factors like traffic patterns, weather conditions, and fuel efficiency, ultimately lowering costs and improving service reliability.

Risk management is another critical area where AI is transforming supply chains. The global nature of modern supply chains makes them increasingly vulnerable to disruptions, such as natural disasters, political instability, or pandemics. AI and machine learning are valuable tools in predicting and mitigating risks by analyzing data from various sources—such as weather reports, geopolitical events, and supplier performance data—to identify potential disruptions. AI-powered systems can simulate various risk scenarios and recommend alternative strategies, allowing businesses to react quickly and minimize the impact of disruptions. For instance, if a key supplier is facing delays due to unforeseen circumstances, AI can identify alternative suppliers or reroute shipments to prevent bottlenecks.

Predictive maintenance is yet another area where AI enhances supply chain performance. Equipment failures in logistics can cause costly delays and operational disruptions. AI-powered predictive maintenance systems monitor supply chain assets—such as trucks, machinery, and warehouse robots—by analyzing sensor data to detect early signs of wear and tear. Machine learning algorithms use this data to predict when equipment is likely to fail, enabling businesses to perform maintenance before breakdowns occur. This proactive approach reduces downtime, extends the lifespan of equipment, and lowers repair costs. For example, a logistics company can use AI to monitor its fleet of delivery trucks, ensuring they are serviced before they experience mechanical failures, thus avoiding delivery delays and improving overall reliability.

AI also enhances the customer experience by offering personalized services. In today's fast-paced, customer-centric world, individuals expect quick and tailored responses. AI-powered chatbots and virtual assistants can provide real-time updates on orders, answer customer queries, and make personal recommendations based on previous purchases. Machine learning algorithms can also analyze customer behavior to predict preferences and offer targeted promotions or product suggestions. This personality not only enhances the customer's experience but also increases brand loyalty and boosts sales. Additionally, AI systems can predict customer preferences for delivery times or packaging, allowing companies to tailor their services to meet individual needs.

Challenges of Implementing AI and Machine Learning in Supply Chains

While the benefits of AI and ML in supply chains are undeniable, their implementation comes with challenges. Some of the most significant obstacles include:

Data Quality and Availability: AI and ML rely heavily on data, and the accuracy of these systems depends on the quality and quantity of data available. Many companies struggle with data silos, where information is fragmented across different systems, making it difficult to harness the full potential of AI.

Cost of Implementation: Developing and implementing AI-powered systems can be costly, especially for small and medium-sized enterprises. The need for advanced infrastructure, skilled personnel, and ongoing maintenance can be a significant barrier to adoption.

Workforce Adaptation: AI and automation can raise concerns about job displacement in traditional supply chain roles. While AI can automate many tasks, it also creates new opportunities for skilled workers in data analysis, AI system management, and strategic decision-making.

Ethical and Legal Concerns: The use of AI raises questions about data privacy, algorithmic transparency, and the ethical use of automation in decision-making. Businesses must navigate these concerns carefully to maintain trust and comply with regulations.

The role of AI and ML in supply chains will continue to grow as these technologies advance. In the future, we can expect AI-driven supply chains that are fully autonomous, and capable of making complex decisions in real-time with minimal human intervention. AI will enable greater levels of collaboration between suppliers, manufacturers, and customers, leading to more efficient and transparent supply chains. As companies continue to invest in AI and ML, the potential for these technologies to drive innovation in logistics and supply chain management is limitless. Businesses that embrace AI today will be better positioned to lead in the competitive global market of tomorrow.

CHAPTER FIVE
Smart Warehousing and Automation

The backbone of modern logistics lies in warehousing. As consumer demand increases and delivery expectations become more stringent, the role of warehouses has shifted from simple storage facilities to dynamic hubs that manage the flow of goods across the supply chain. In this chapter, we'll explore how smart warehousing and automation are revolutionizing the way businesses manage inventory, fulfil orders, and optimize efficiency in the logistics sector.

The Evolution of Warehousing

Traditionally, warehouses were static locations where goods were stored for extended periods before being dispatched. The efficiency of these operations depended on manual labor and basic management systems. However, as global trade expanded and consumer expectations shifted toward faster deliveries, the need for more agile and efficient warehousing operations became clear. The emergence of e-commerce further intensified the pressure on warehouses. With millions of items being purchased online every day, fulfilment centers must now manage complex tasks such as picking, packing, and shipping orders at high speed. This is where smart warehousing and automation technologies come into play.

What is a Smart Warehouse?

A smart warehouse is a facility where advanced technologies—such as robotics, artificial intelligence (AI), the Internet of Things (IoT), and data analytics—are used to automate and optimize various processes. These technologies enable warehouses to operate with minimal human intervention, resulting in faster, more accurate, and more efficient order fulfilment. Smart warehouses go beyond traditional automation by integrating systems that can communicate with each other, learn from data, and make real-time decisions. This interconnectedness allows businesses to adapt to fluctuations in demand, optimize inventory management, and streamline operations across the supply chain.

Robotics in Warehousing

Robotics has been one of the most transformative technologies in modern warehousing. Robots are increasingly being used to perform tasks that were once labor-intensive and time-consuming, such as:

Picking and Packing: Autonomous robots can navigate through warehouses to locate and retrieve items for orders. These robots are equipped with advanced sensors and AI algorithms that allow them to move efficiently, avoid obstacles, and handle products delicately.

Sorting: Robots can sort items based on size, weight, or destination, streamlining the packaging and shipping process. This significantly reduces human error and speeds up order fulfilment.

Loading and Unloading: Robotic arms and conveyor systems are used to load and unload goods from trucks, minimizing manual labor and reducing the risk of injury for workers.

The use of robotics not only increases efficiency but also allows warehouses to scale up operations during peak periods, such as holidays, without relying on additional human labor.

The Internet of Things (IoT) for Real-Time Tracking

The Internet of Things (IoT) plays a crucial role in enabling real-time tracking and monitoring within smart warehouses. IoT devices, such as sensors and RFID tags, are embedded in goods, pallets, and equipment to provide real-time data on location, movement, and condition. This real-time visibility allows warehouse managers to monitor inventory levels, track shipments, and ensure that goods are stored in optimal conditions. For example, temperature-sensitive items can be monitored throughout the storage and transportation process, ensuring that they remain within the required temperature range. IoT also enables predictive maintenance for warehouse equipment. Sensors can detect wear and tear in machinery and send alerts when maintenance is needed, reducing downtime and ensuring that operations continue without disruption.

AI and Data Analytics in Warehousing

Artificial intelligence (AI) and data analytics are fundamental to the smart warehouse's ability to optimize processes and make data-driven decisions. AI systems analyze vast amounts of data collected from IoT devices, robotic systems, and warehouse management software to identify patterns and make recommendations for improvement.

Some key applications of AI and data analytics in warehousing include:

Optimizing Warehouse Layouts: AI systems can analyze order data to determine the most efficient layout for the warehouse. By placing frequently ordered items in easily accessible locations, businesses can reduce the time it takes to pick and pack orders.

Demand Forecasting: AI-powered demand forecasting tools analyze historical sales data, market trends, and other factors to predict future demand. This enables warehouses to optimize inventory levels, ensuring they have the right amount of stock on hand while minimizing excess inventory.

Resource Allocation: Data analytics can identify inefficiencies in resource allocation, such as labor or equipment usage. By analyzing workflows, businesses can make informed decisions about where to allocate resources for maximum productivity.

Automated Storage and Retrieval Systems (ASRS)

Automated Storage and Retrieval Systems (ASRS) are highly advanced systems that use automation to store and retrieve goods from designated storage areas. These systems are typically made up of cranes, conveyors, and shuttles that move goods between storage racks and retrieval points. ASRS allows warehouses to maximize the use of vertical space, storing goods in compact areas that would be difficult for human workers to access. This technology not only increases storage capacity but also speeds up the retrieval process, as items can be automatically brought to workers or robots for picking and packing. ASRS is particularly useful in high-volume fulfilment centers, where speed and accuracy are critical. By automating the storage and retrieval process, businesses can fulfil orders faster while reducing labor costs and human error.

Automation in Order Fulfillment

In addition to storage and retrieval, automation is playing a key role in transforming the order fulfilment process. With the rise in e-commerce, warehouses must be able to process orders quickly and accurately, often handling thousands of items each day. Automated order fulfillment systems can handle the entire process from receiving an order to packing it for shipment. These systems use AI to optimize the picking process, ensuring that items are retrieved in the most efficient sequence. Once items are picked, they are automatically packed and labelled for shipping. In some fulfilment centers, automated guided vehicles (AGVs) transport goods between different areas of the warehouse, further streamlining the order fulfilment process.

Autonomous Drones and Inventory Audits

Another emerging technology in smart warehousing is the use of autonomous drones to conduct inventory audits. In traditional warehouses, inventory audits are time-consuming and labor-intensive, requiring workers to manually count and verify stock levels. Autonomous drones equipped with cameras and sensors can fly through warehouses, scanning barcodes or RFID tags to count inventory. This process is significantly faster and more accurate than manual audits, and it can be conducted without disrupting warehouse operations. Drones are particularly useful in large warehouses with high shelves that are difficult for workers to access. By automating the inventory audit process, businesses can ensure accurate inventory records while freeing up workers for other tasks.

Benefits of Smart Warehousing and Automation

The adoption of smart warehousing and automation technologies offers numerous benefits for businesses, including:

Increased Efficiency: Automation reduces the time it takes to fulfil orders, process inventory, and manage resources, resulting in faster turnaround times and improved customer satisfaction.

Improved Accuracy: Automated systems are less prone to errors than manual processes, leading to fewer mistakes in picking, packing, and inventory management.

Cost Savings: While the initial investment in automation technology can be high, the long-term savings in labor costs, storage space, and operational efficiency make it a worthwhile investment.

Scalability: Smart warehouses can easily scale operations up or down based on demand, allowing businesses to handle peak periods without adding significant labor costs.

Enhanced Safety: By automating dangerous or repetitive tasks, smart warehouses reduce the risk of injury to human workers, creating a safer work environment.

Challenges and Considerations

While smart warehousing offers significant advantages, there are challenges that businesses must consider when implementing these technologies:

High Initial Costs: The investment required to implement smart warehousing technologies can be significant, particularly for smaller businesses. However, the long-term benefits often outweigh the upfront costs.

Integration with Legacy Systems: Many warehouses still rely on outdated systems that may not be compatible with modern automation technologies. Businesses must ensure that their existing infrastructure can support new technologies.

Workforce Transition: As automation replaces manual tasks, companies must invest in training workers to manage and operate these advanced systems. This shift in skill requirements may lead to workforce challenges.

The Future of Smart Warehousing

The future of warehousing is undeniably smart. As technologies like AI, robotics, and IoT continue to advance, warehouses will become even more autonomous, and capable of managing operations with minimal human oversight. Autonomous vehicles, drones, and AI-powered systems will play increasingly prominent roles in the supply chain, improving efficiency and flexibility at every stage. Companies that invest in smart warehousing today will be better positioned to meet the demands of tomorrow's logistics landscape. The ability to fulfil orders quickly, accurately, and efficiently will become a key differentiator in the competitive world of e-commerce and global trade.

CHAPTER SIX
Blockchain and Supply Chain Transparency.

I n today's interconnected global economy, the demand for transparency in supply chains has never been greater. Consumers want to know the origins of their products, businesses need assurance about the authenticity of their materials, and governments enforce regulations to ensure ethical practices and environmental compliance. Blockchain technology has emerged as a groundbreaking solution to these challenges, offering a secure, immutable, and transparent way to record, verify, and share information across the supply chain. This chapter explores how blockchain transforms supply chain management, its real-world applications, and the numerous benefits it offers for transparency, security, and operational efficiency.

Understanding Blockchain Technology

Blockchain is often described as a decentralized, distributed ledger that records transactions across a network of computers, ensuring transparency, security, and immutability. At its core, blockchain operates on the principle of a shared, trusted record-keeping system where data is stored in "blocks." Each block contains a set of transactions and is linked to the previous block through cryptographic hashes, forming a continuous chain of information. This creates a tamper-proof, chronological ledger that all participants in the network can trust. A key feature of blockchain is that it operates on a decentralized network. Unlike traditional centralized databases, where a single entity controls the data, blockchain relies on a network of computers (or nodes), each holding a copy of the entire ledger. Changes to the ledger can only be made if the majority of nodes reach a consensus, making it nearly impossible for a single party to alter or falsify the data. This ensures a high level of security, transparency, and trust—critical factors in managing global supply chains. Originally developed to power cryptocurrencies like Bitcoin, blockchain's potential has expanded far beyond digital currency. Industries such as finance, healthcare, real estate, and, most notably, supply chain management have begun adopting blockchain to address key challenges and create more efficient, transparent systems.

The Need for Transparency in Supply Chains

Supply chain transparency refers to the ability to trace the movement of goods and verify their authenticity, origin, and condition as they move from suppliers to manufacturers, distributors, and eventually to consumers. In traditional supply chains, this process is often opaque, with little visibility in the intermediate steps. Companies rely on third-party intermediaries, manual processes, and paper documentation, which can lead to inefficiencies, errors, and even fraudulent activities.

Transparency in supply chains is becoming increasingly important for a couple of reasons:

Counterfeiting and Fraud Prevention: Counterfeiting is a pervasive problem, particularly in industries like pharmaceuticals, luxury goods, and electronics. Without proper verification, counterfeit goods can easily enter the supply chain, jeopardizing consumer safety and brand integrity.

Regulatory Compliance: Governments and industry bodies are introducing stricter regulations to ensure products meet specific environmental, safety, and ethical standards. Businesses must prove that their supply chains comply with these regulations, often requiring detailed documentation and audits.

Blockchain addresses these challenges by providing an immutable, verifiable record of every transaction and movement of goods within the supply chain. By offering real-time visibility and accountability, blockchain ensures that businesses, consumers, and regulatory bodies have access to accurate, reliable data at all times.

Key Features of Blockchain for Supply Chain Transparency

Blockchain brings several key features to the table that make it ideal for enhancing transparency in supply chains:

Immutability: Once data is recorded on the blockchain, it cannot be altered or deleted. This ensures that the information is secure, permanent, and trustworthy. All parties can be confident that the data has not been tampered with, and any attempt to manipulate the ledger would require consensus from the majority of the network's nodes, which is highly unlikely.

Decentralization: Blockchain operates on a decentralized network, meaning no single party has control over the data. These fosters trust between supply chain participants, as all stakeholders have access to the same information and can verify it independently.

Real-Time Tracking and Traceability: Blockchain enables real-time tracking of goods throughout the supply chain. Each transaction, from sourcing raw materials to final delivery, is recorded on the blockchain, providing full traceability. Businesses can monitor the status and location of goods at every stage, allowing for quick responses to potential disruptions or delays.

Smart Contracts: Blockchain supports smart contracts, which are self-executing contracts with terms and conditions directly written into code. These contracts automatically trigger actions (such as payments or approvals) when certain conditions are met, eliminating the need for intermediaries and ensuring more efficient, transparent transactions.

Real-World Applications for Blockchain in Supply Chains

Blockchain's potential to enhance transparency and security in supply chains is already being realized in a variety of industries. Below are some key real-world applications that demonstrate the transformative power of blockchain technology:

a. Traceability of Goods and Authenticity Verification:

Blockchain's ability to track goods from their origin to their final destination is particularly valuable in industries that require strict quality control and authenticity verification, such as food, pharmaceuticals, and luxury goods. By using blockchain, companies can create a digital trail that verifies the authenticity and quality of products at each stage of the supply chain. For example, in the food industry, blockchain can track the journey of food products from farm to table. Companies like Walmart and Nestlé have implemented blockchain-based traceability systems to monitor the origin, processing, and transportation of food items. This ensures that consumers can verify the source of their products and that retailers can quickly trace any food safety issues, such as contamination or recalls. Similarly, in the pharmaceutical industry, blockchain is being used to combat the problem of counterfeit drugs. Pharmaceutical companies can assign unique identifiers to each batch of medication, which are recorded on the blockchain. This allows pharmacists and consumers to verify the authenticity of the drugs they receive, reducing the risk of counterfeit products entering the market.

b. Fighting Counterfeiting in Luxury Goods

Counterfeiting is a major concern for the luxury goods industry, where high-value products like designer handbags, watches, and jeweler are often targeted by counterfeiters. Blockchain provides a solution by enabling brands to create digital certificates of authenticity that are recorded on the blockchain. Each product can be assigned a unique digital identity, which is linked to its physical counterpart. As the product moves through the supply chain, every transaction is recorded on the blockchain, creating a permanent, tamper-proof record. Consumers can scan a QR code or use an app to verify the authenticity of the product, ensuring that they are purchasing genuine items. Brands such as Louis Vuitton and LVMH are exploring blockchain solutions to enhance the traceability and authenticity of their luxury products, protecting their brand reputation and providing consumers with peace of mind.

c. Ethical Sourcing and Sustainability Initiatives

In an era where consumers are increasingly demanding ethical and sustainable products, blockchain offers a way for companies to prove their commitment to these values. By providing transparent, verifiable records of sourcing practices, blockchain enables businesses to demonstrate that their products are sourced responsibly. For example, blockchain can be used to trace the journey of raw materials like cotton, coffee, or palm oil, ensuring that they are sourced from suppliers who meet ethical labor and environmental standards. This level of transparency is particularly valuable in industries like fashion and agriculture, where concerns about child labor, deforestation, and environmental degradation are prevalent. Unilever, for example, has implemented a blockchain-based platform to track the sustainability of its palm oil supply chain. By using blockchain, Unilever can verify that its suppliers are adhering to sustainability standards, such as protecting biodiversity and reducing deforestation, and share this information with consumers and stakeholders.

d. Regulatory Compliance and Documentation

Complying with regulations in industries such as food, pharmaceuticals, and chemicals often requires extensive documentation and verification. Blockchain simplifies this process by providing a transparent, immutable record of compliance with industry standards and regulations. In the seafood industry, for instance, blockchain is being used to ensure that fish are sourced sustainably and in accordance with environmental regulations. Blockchain can track the entire journey of fish, from the point of capture to the final sale, ensuring compliance with safety, sustainability, and legal requirements. Additionally, blockchain can streamline the auditing process by providing regulators with direct access to supply chain data. This reduces the need for manual audits and paperwork, speeding up the process of verifying compliance with industry standards.

Enhancing Supply Chain Security with Blockchain

Blockchain's decentralized and immutable nature provides a high level of security, making it an ideal solution for protecting sensitive supply chain data. Traditional centralized systems are vulnerable to hacking, fraud, and data manipulation, as they rely on a single point of control. In contrast, blockchain's distributed ledger ensures that data is stored across multiple nodes, making it highly resistant to tampering. Additionally, blockchain's use of cryptographic techniques ensures that data is encrypted and secure, preventing unauthorized access. This level of security is particularly valuable for protecting sensitive information, such as intellectual property, confidential agreements, or financial transactions.

Blockchain-Enabled Collaboration and Trust in Supply Chains

One of blockchain's most transformative impacts on supply chains is its ability to foster collaboration and trust between all participants. In traditional supply chains, transactions and records are often siloed, with each party maintaining its own version of the truth. This can lead to disputes, delays, and inefficiencies. With blockchain, all participants in the supply chain—suppliers, manufacturers, distributors, retailers, and even consumers—have access to the same, transparent record of transactions. This eliminates the need for intermediaries, reduces the risk of disputes, and fosters a higher level of trust and collaboration. For example, a supplier can record the delivery of raw materials on the blockchain, and the manufacturer can verify the quality and authenticity of the materials before accepting them. This transparency ensures that all parties are held accountable for their actions, leading to more efficient and trustworthy supply chain operations.

Challenges of Implementing Blockchain in Supply Chains

While the benefits of blockchain are clear, implementing the technology in supply chains presents several challenges:

High Initial Costs: Developing and deploying a blockchain-based solution requires significant investment in infrastructure, technology, and training. Small and medium-sized enterprises (SMEs) may find it challenging to adopt blockchain due to the high upfront costs.

Integration with Legacy Systems: Most businesses already use a variety of software systems to manage their supply chains. Integrating blockchain with these existing systems can be complex and time-consuming. Companies need to ensure that blockchain solutions can seamlessly work with their current technology stack.

Scalability Issues: Blockchain's decentralized nature, while secure, can lead to slower processing times and scalability issues, particularly when dealing with large volumes of transactions. Businesses must carefully assess whether blockchain can handle the scale and complexity of their supply chains.

Regulatory Uncertainty: Blockchain is still a relatively new technology, and the regulatory environment surrounding its use is evolving. Companies must stay informed about potential legal and regulatory challenges related to data privacy, security, and compliance.

Blockchain in Supply Chain Management

As blockchain technology continues to evolve and mature, its adoption in supply chain management is expected to grow. The ability to provide an immutable, decentralized, and transparent record of transactions will become increasingly important as supply chains become more complex and globalized. In the future, we can expect to see blockchain integrated with other emerging technologies, such as artificial intelligence (AI) and the Internet of Things (IoT), to create fully transparent, automated supply chains. This will enable businesses to make real-time decisions, optimize operations, and build greater trust with consumers and stakeholders. Companies that invest in blockchain today will be better positioned to navigate the complexities of tomorrow's global economy, ensuring that their supply chains are secure, transparent, and efficient.

CHAPTER SEVEN
The Role of Data Analytics in Decision-Making

Data is often referred to as the "new oil" in today's digital economy, and nowhere is this more evident than in supply chain management. As supply chains become more complex and globalized, businesses are increasingly turning to data analytics to drive decision-making, optimize operations, and gain a competitive edge. In this chapter, we will explore how data analytics is transforming supply chains, the key technologies behind it, and how companies can harness the power of data to make more informed, strategic decisions.

Understanding Data Analytics in Supply Chains

At its core, data analytics involves the process of collecting, analyzing, and interpreting large sets of data to uncover patterns, trends, and insights. These insights can then be used to improve decision-making, optimize processes, and predict future outcomes. In the context of supply chain management, data analytics provides real-time visibility into every aspect of the supply chain, from inventory levels and demand forecasting to transportation routes and supplier performance.

Data analytics can be divided into four key types, each offering different levels of insight:

Descriptive Analytics: Provides a summary of past and current supply chain data, answering the question, "What happened?"

Diagnostic Analytics: Delves deeper into data to determine the reasons behind past outcomes, answering the question, "Why did it happen?"

Predictive Analytics: Uses historical data and statistical algorithms to forecast future trends and outcomes, answering the question, "What is likely to happen?"

Prescriptive Analytics: Suggests actions or decisions based on predictive insights, answering the question, "What should we do?"

The Power of Predictive Analytics in Demand Forecasting

One of the most significant applications of data analytics in supply chain management is demand forecasting. In traditional supply chains, demand forecasting was often based on historical sales data and market trends. However, this approach was limited in its accuracy, leading to overstocking, stockouts, and inefficiencies. Predictive analytics revolutionizes demand forecasting by using machine learning algorithms and large datasets to predict future demand with a high degree of accuracy. These algorithms analyze a wide range of factors, including historical sales data, market trends, economic indicators, and even external factors such as weather patterns and social media sentiment.

By identifying patterns and correlations in the data, predictive analytics can provide businesses with accurate forecasts of future demand. For example, an e-commerce company can use predictive analytics to anticipate spikes in demand during holiday seasons or promotional events. By adjusting inventory levels and production schedules accordingly, the company can avoid stockouts and ensure that products are available when customers need them.

Additionally, predictive analytics can help companies respond to unexpected changes in demand, such as those caused by natural disasters, pandemics, or geopolitical events. This agility allows businesses to maintain service levels and avoid disruptions in the supply chain.

Inventory Optimization Through Data-Driven Insights

Effective inventory management is critical to the success of any supply chain. Businesses must strike a delicate balance between holding enough inventory to meet customer demand and minimizing excess stock, which ties up capital and increases carrying costs. Data analytics provides the tools needed to achieve this balance through inventory optimization. By analyzing historical sales data, lead times, and demand patterns, data analytics can help businesses determine the optimal inventory levels for each product. This ensures that inventory is available when needed while minimizing the risk of overstocking or understocking. For example, a retailer can use data analytics to analyze purchasing patterns and determine which products are in high demand during specific times of the year. By adjusting inventory levels based on these insights, the retailer can reduce carrying costs while ensuring that popular items are always in stock. In addition, data analytics can improve safety stock management by analyzing the variability in demand and lead times. By calculating the optimal amount of safety stock needed to buffer against fluctuations in demand, businesses can reduce the risk of stockouts and maintain high service levels.

Route Optimization and Transportation Efficiency

Transportation and logistics are critical components of the supply chain, and data analytics plays a key role in optimizing transportation routes and improving overall efficiency. Route optimization uses real-time data, such as traffic conditions, weather patterns, and delivery schedules, to determine the most efficient routes for shipments. This minimizes fuel consumption, reduces transportation costs, and ensures timely deliveries. For example, a logistics company can use data analytics to track the location of its delivery trucks in real time and identify the fastest, most efficient routes for each delivery. By factoring in variables such as traffic congestion, road closures, and weather conditions, the company can optimize its routes, reducing fuel consumption and delivery times. In addition to route optimization, data analytics can improve transportation planning by analyzing historical shipping data and identifying patterns in delivery times, delays, and transportation costs. This enables businesses to make more informed decisions about carrier selection, transportation modes, and shipping schedules, ultimately improving the efficiency of their logistics operations.

Supplier Performance Management and Risk Mitigation

Supply chain disruptions caused by supplier issues can have significant consequences for businesses, leading to delays, increased costs, and lost sales. Supplier performance management is essential for mitigating these risks and ensuring the smooth operation of the supply chain. Data analytics provides the tools needed to monitor supplier performance, identify potential risks, and take proactive measures to address them. By analyzing supplier data—such as lead times, on-time delivery rates, quality metrics, and pricing trends, businesses can assess the reliability and performance of their suppliers. This enables them to identify high-performing suppliers and develop stronger relationships with them, while also flagging underperforming suppliers that may pose a risk to the supply chain.

For example, a manufacturer can use data analytics to monitor the performance of its raw material suppliers and identify any patterns of late deliveries or quality issues. If a supplier consistently underperforms, the manufacturer can take corrective actions, such as renegotiating contracts or switching to alternative suppliers, to minimize the impact on production schedules. In addition, data analytics can be used to predict and mitigate supply chain risks. By analyzing external data sources—such as geopolitical events, natural disasters, or financial instability, businesses can identify potential risks to their supply chain and develop contingency plans to address them. This proactive approach helps businesses avoid costly disruptions and maintain continuity in their operations.

Real-Time Decision-Making with Data Analytics

One of the most powerful aspects of data analytics is its ability to provide real-time insights that enable businesses to make quick, informed decisions. In the fast-paced world of supply chain management, delays in decision-making can lead to missed opportunities, inefficiencies, and disruptions. With the advent of real-time data analytics platforms, businesses can now monitor key performance indicators (KPIs) in real-time, such as inventory levels, order fulfilment rates, transportation costs, and customer satisfaction metrics. This allows supply chain managers to identify issues as they arise and take immediate action to resolve them. For example, a retailer can use real-time data analytics to monitor the status of orders as they are processed and shipped.

If the system detects a delay in a shipment, the retailer can reroute the delivery or notify the customer of the delay, ensuring that customer expectations are managed effectively. Real-time data analytics also enables dynamic decision-making, allowing businesses to adjust their strategies based on changing conditions. For example, if a sudden surge in demand is detected for a particular product, a company can automatically adjust its production schedule, allocate more resources to that product, and update inventory levels in real time to meet the increased demand.

Enhancing Customer Experience with Data Analytics

In addition to improving operational efficiency, data analytics plays a key role in enhancing the customer experience. By analyzing customer behavior, preferences, and purchasing patterns, businesses can tailor their supply chain operations to meet customer needs more effectively. For example, e-commerce companies can use data analytics to offer personalized product recommendations, optimize delivery windows, and improve order fulfilment accuracy. By understanding customer preferences and anticipating their needs, businesses can create a more seamless and satisfying customer experience. In addition, data analytics can be used to predict and prevent customer dissatisfaction by identifying potential issues in the supply chain before they impact customers. For example, if data analytics detects a delay in shipping due to a transportation issue, the company can proactively notify customers and offer alternative solutions, such as expedited shipping or discounts on future orders. By using data analytics to improve the customer experience, businesses can build stronger relationships with their customers, increase loyalty, and drive repeat business.

Challenges of Implementing Data Analytics in Supply Chains

While the benefits of data analytics in supply chain management are clear, there are several challenges that businesses must address when implementing these technologies:

Data Quality and Integration: The accuracy of data analytics depends on the quality of the data being analyzed. Many companies struggle with data silos, where information is fragmented across different systems and departments. Integrating data from multiple sources and ensuring its accuracy is critical to the success of data analytics initiatives.

Cost of Implementation: Developing and maintaining data analytics systems can be expensive, particularly for small and medium-sized enterprises (SMEs). The cost of collecting, storing, and analyzing large volumes of data, as well as investing in the necessary technology and expertise, can be a barrier to adoption.

Skill Gaps: Data analytics requires specialized skills, such as data science, statistical analysis, and machine learning. Many companies face challenges in finding and retaining employees with the expertise needed to implement and manage data analytics systems.

Data Security and Privacy: As businesses collect and analyze vast amounts of data, they must ensure that sensitive information is protected from unauthorized access or breaches. Implementing robust data security and privacy measures is essential to maintaining trust and compliance with regulations.

Data Analytics in Supply Chains

The role of data analytics in supply chain management will only continue to grow as businesses recognize the value of data-driven decision-making. In the future, we can expect to see even more advanced applications of data analytics, including the integration of artificial intelligence (AI) and machine learning to automate decision-making processes and optimize supply chain operations in real time. As businesses continue to invest in data analytics, the potential for improved efficiency, reduced costs, and enhanced customer satisfaction is limitless. Companies that embrace data analytics as a core component of their supply chain strategy will be better positioned to thrive in an increasingly competitive global market.

CHAPTER EIGHT
Sustainable Supply Chains with Technology

As global concerns about climate change, environmental degradation, and resource scarcity intensify, sustainability has become a key priority for businesses worldwide. Supply chains, often considered the backbone of the global economy, are under pressure to adopt more sustainable practices. To achieve this, companies are increasingly turning to advanced technologies that can help them optimize resource use, reduce waste, and minimize their environmental impact. In this chapter, we explore how technology is driving sustainability in supply chains and how businesses can balance operational efficiency with environmental responsibility.

The Importance of Sustainability in Supply Chains

Sustainability in supply chains refers to the practice of managing and optimizing the flow of goods, services, and information in ways that minimize the environmental impact and promote social and economic responsibility. A sustainable supply chain seeks to reduce waste, conserve resources, lower carbon emissions, and ensure ethical labor practices throughout the entire process—from sourcing raw materials to delivering finished goods to consumers.

Sustainable supply chains are no longer a niche concern; they have become essential for companies across industries. This shift is driven by several factors:

Consumer Demand: Today's consumers are more environmentally conscious and are demanding products that are ethically sourced, sustainably produced, and delivered with minimal environmental impact. Businesses that fail to meet these expectations risk losing market share and damaging their reputation.

Regulatory Pressure: Governments around the world are introducing stricter environmental regulations and sustainability standards. Companies are required to comply with laws related to carbon emissions, waste disposal, water usage, and fair labor practices, among others.

Operational Efficiency: Sustainability is not just about reducing environmental impact; it's also about improving efficiency. By optimizing the use of resources, reducing waste, and minimizing inefficiencies, businesses can cut costs and improve their bottom line while also contributing to a more sustainable future.

Investor Expectations: Investors are increasingly factoring sustainability into their decision-making process. Companies that demonstrate strong environmental, social, and governance (ESG) performance are more likely to attract investment and build long-term value.

Using Data Analytics and AI to Drive Sustainability

Data analytics and artificial intelligence (AI) are critical tools for helping companies achieve sustainability in their supply chains. By analyzing vast amounts of data, businesses can identify inefficiencies, predict future resource needs, and optimize processes to reduce environmental impact.

Energy Efficiency: AI-powered systems can analyze energy usage data in factories, warehouses, and transportation networks to identify areas where energy consumption can be reduced. For example, AI can suggest optimal times for running energy-intensive equipment to minimize electricity usage during peak hours or adjust heating and cooling systems to reduce energy waste.

Resource Optimization: Data analytics can help companies optimize the use of raw materials and reduce waste. By analyzing production processes, AI can identify areas where materials are being overused or wasted and recommend changes to reduce resource consumption. This can lead to more sustainable production practices and reduce the environmental impact of manufacturing.

Predictive Maintenance: AI and machine learning can be used to monitor the condition of machinery and equipment, predicting when maintenance is required. By ensuring that equipment operates efficiently, businesses can reduce energy consumption, extend the life of their machinery, and avoid unplanned downtime that could lead to increased environmental impact.

IoT and Real-Time Monitoring for Environmental Impact

The Internet of Things (IoT) plays a crucial role in enabling real-time monitoring of environmental conditions throughout the supply chain. IoT devices equipped with sensors can track energy consumption, water usage, waste generation, and carbon emissions in real-time, allowing businesses to make data-driven decisions to reduce their environmental impact.

Carbon Footprint Tracking: IoT sensors can monitor the carbon emissions generated by transportation, production processes, and facilities. By collecting real-time data on emissions, businesses can identify areas where carbon output can be reduced, such as optimizing transportation routes to minimize fuel consumption or adjusting production processes to lower emissions.

Water and Waste Management: IoT devices can track water usage in manufacturing plants and other facilities, helping businesses identify areas where water can be conserved. In addition, IoT can be used to monitor waste production and recycling rates, ensuring that waste is minimized and properly managed.

Supply Chain Visibility: IoT devices provide visibility into every stage of the supply chain, from sourcing raw materials to delivering products to consumers. This visibility allows businesses to track the environmental impact of each step in the supply chain and take corrective actions to reduce resource consumption and waste.

For example, a food manufacturer can use IoT sensors to monitor water usage in its processing plants and optimize water consumption to reduce waste. The company can also track the environmental impact of its suppliers, ensuring that they meet sustainability standards.

Blockchain for Sustainable Supply Chain Transparency

As discussed in Chapter 6, blockchain technology offers unparalleled transparency and traceability in supply chains. This is particularly valuable for ensuring that products are sourced and produced sustainably. By recording every transaction and movement of goods on an immutable ledger, blockchain enables companies to verify the environmental and ethical credentials of their suppliers and ensure that sustainability standards are met at every stage.

Sustainable Sourcing: Blockchain can be used to trace the journey of raw materials, such as coffee, cotton, or palm oil, from the point of origin to the final product. This ensures that materials are sourced from suppliers that adhere to environmental and ethical standards, such as minimizing deforestation, reducing water usage, or promoting fair labor practices.

Reducing Waste in the Supply Chain: Blockchain can help minimize waste by improving supply chain coordination and reducing inefficiencies. For example, by providing real-time visibility into inventory levels and demand, blockchain can prevent overproduction and excess inventory, reducing the amount of waste generated by unsold or expired products.

Verifying Carbon Offsets: Blockchain can be used to verify the authenticity of carbon offsets, ensuring that businesses are genuinely reducing their carbon emissions. This transparency helps companies meet their sustainability goals and provide proof to regulators, investors, and consumers that their carbon reduction efforts are legitimate.

Sustainable Transportation and Logistics with Automation

The transportation and logistics sector is one of the largest contributors to carbon emissions in supply chains. However, technology is playing a significant role in reducing the environmental impact of transportation through automation, route optimization, and the adoption of electric and alternative fuel vehicles.

Route Optimization: Data analytics and AI can optimize transportation routes to minimize fuel consumption and reduce emissions. By analyzing traffic patterns, delivery schedules, and road conditions, AI-powered route optimization tools can identify the most efficient routes for shipments, reducing both fuel use and delivery times.

Electric and Autonomous Vehicles: The adoption of electric vehicles (EVs) and autonomous vehicles in logistics is another important step toward sustainable transportation. EVs produce zero tailpipe emissions, making them an environmentally friendly alternative to traditional diesel-powered trucks. Autonomous vehicles, powered by AI, can further reduce emissions by optimizing driving behavior and reducing fuel consumption.

Drones for Last-Mile Delivery: Drones are emerging as a viable solution for reducing the environmental impact of last-mile deliveries. By using drones for local deliveries, businesses can reduce the number of delivery trucks on the road, cutting emissions and fuel consumption. Drones are especially useful in urban areas where traffic congestion can increase delivery times and emissions.

Circular Supply Chains and the Role of Technology

Circular supply chains focus on the principles of reuse, recycling, and reducing waste by keeping materials and products in circulation for as long as possible. Technology plays a vital role in enabling circular supply chains by improving resource recovery, recycling processes, and product lifecycle management.

Product Lifecycle Management (PLM): Data analytics, IoT, and blockchain can be used to track the lifecycle of products from manufacturing to end-of-life. This visibility allows businesses to identify opportunities for product reuse, refurbishment, or recycling. For example, a manufacturer can use IoT sensors to track the condition of its products in use and determine when they can be returned for refurbishment or recycling.

Recycling and Waste Reduction: AI-powered systems can improve recycling processes by identifying materials that can be reused or recycled, reducing the amount of waste sent to landfills. For example, AI can analyze the composition of waste and sort materials more accurately, improving recycling rates and reducing contamination.

Product-as-a-Service Models: Technology enables the shift from traditional ownership models to product-as-a-service models, where businesses retain ownership of products and lease them to customers. This encourages manufacturers to design products that are durable, repairable, and recyclable, reducing waste and promoting sustainability.

For example, in the electronics industry, companies like HP and Dell offer product-as-a-service models where customers lease printers or computers instead of buying them outright. At the end of the product's lifecycle, the company recovers the device for refurbishment or recycling, reducing e-waste and promoting a circular economy.

Challenges of Implementing Sustainable Supply Chains

While technology provides powerful tools for achieving sustainability in supply chains, there are several challenges that businesses must overcome:

Cost of Adoption: Implementing sustainable technologies, such as electric vehicles, IoT devices, and blockchain, can be expensive. The upfront investment required to adopt these technologies may be a barrier for smaller companies, even though the long-term benefits often outweigh the initial costs.

Integration with Existing Systems: Many businesses operate legacy systems that are not easily compatible with modern sustainable technologies. Integrating these technologies into the existing supply chain infrastructure can be complex and time-consuming.

Supplier Compliance: Achieving sustainability in supply chains often requires collaboration with suppliers, who may not always be willing or able to meet the required sustainability standards. Ensuring supplier compliance with sustainability goals can be a challenge, especially for businesses with complex, global supply chains.

The Future of Sustainable Supply Chains

The future of supply chains is undeniably green. As technology continues to advance, businesses will have even more tools at their disposal to reduce their environmental impact, optimize resource use, and meet the growing demand for sustainable products. Companies that embrace these technologies and integrate sustainability into their supply chain strategies will not only reduce their environmental footprint but also enhance their competitiveness in a rapidly changing global market. In the coming years, we can expect to see greater adoption of AI, IoT, and blockchain in sustainable supply chains, as well as increased use of renewable energy, circular economy practices, and low-emission transportation options. Sustainability will no longer be a "nice-to-have" but a core component of business strategy, driven by both consumer demand and regulatory requirements. Businesses that take proactive steps to adopt sustainable technologies and practices today will be better positioned to thrive in the future, while contributing to a healthier planet for generations to come.

CHAPTER NINE
Challenges and Risks in Adopting Logistics 4.0

While the benefits of Logistics 4.0 are undeniable—improved efficiency, real-time visibility, automation, and greater transparency—businesses often face significant challenges when implementing these technologies. Adopting Logistics 4.0 is not just about integrating cutting-edge solutions; it requires a fundamental shift in how supply chains are managed, how data is utilized, and how teams are organized. In this chapter, we will explore the key challenges and risks that companies face when transitioning to Logistics 4.0, and how they can navigate these obstacles to ensure a successful digital transformation.

High Initial Costs and Investment Requirements

One of the most significant barriers to adopting Logistics 4.0 technologies is the high upfront costs associated with implementing new systems, hardware, and infrastructure. Technologies such as robotics, AI-powered analytics platforms, IoT devices, and blockchain often require substantial financial investment, especially for small and medium-sized enterprises (SMEs). Hardware and Equipment Costs: Automation technologies, such as robotics and automated storage and retrieval systems (ASRS), come with hefty price tags. Businesses need to invest in specialized equipment, sensors, and devices to enable real-time tracking, automation, and data collection. Software and Integration Costs: Implementing AI-powered platforms, predictive analytics tools, and blockchain requires significant investment in software. Moreover, integrating these solutions with existing enterprise resource planning (ERP) systems or warehouse management systems (WMS) can be complex and expensive.

Training and Skill Development: Beyond the financial cost of purchasing technology, companies also need to invest in training their workforce to operate and manage new systems. As Logistics 4.0 introduces automation, AI, and other advanced technologies, businesses need a skilled workforce that understands how to leverage these tools effectively. For many companies, particularly those with limited budgets, the financial commitment required to adopt Logistics 4.0 can be a significant obstacle. However, businesses should also consider the long-term return on investment (ROI) that these technologies can provide. Automation, real-time data, and AI-driven decision-making have the potential to significantly reduce operational costs, increase productivity, and improve supply chain resilience, ultimately making the initial investment worthwhile.

Integration with Legacy Systems

One of the most complex challenges in adopting Logistics 4.0 is integrating new technologies with legacy systems, the older, often outdated software and hardware systems that many businesses still rely on to manage their supply chains. Legacy systems were not designed to handle the level of connectivity, data, and automation required for Logistics 4.0, making integration a daunting task.

Compatibility Issues: Legacy systems may not be compatible with modern technologies such as IoT devices, AI platforms, or blockchain. This creates a barrier to achieving real-time data sharing, process automation, and end-to-end visibility across the supply chain.

Data Silos: Many companies operate in Silos, with different departments using separate software systems to manage operations. These systems often do not communicate effectively with one another, leading to data fragmentation. Logistics 4.0 requires an integrated, connected approach where data flows seamlessly across the supply chain. Breaking down these silos is a significant challenge.

Migration Risks: Transitioning from legacy systems to modern technologies can be a risky process. Data loss, system downtime, and business disruptions are all potential risks during migration. Businesses must plan carefully to minimize these risks and ensure a smooth transition.

To overcome these challenges, companies need to invest in integration solutions that can connect legacy systems with modern technologies. This may involve the use of middleware or application programming interfaces (APIs) to enable data sharing and communication between different platforms. Additionally, businesses should adopt a phased approach to migration, gradually transitioning from legacy systems to Logistics 4.0 technologies to minimize disruption.

Cybersecurity Risks

As supply chains become increasingly digital and interconnected, the risk of cybersecurity threats also grows. Logistics 4.0 relies on the seamless flow of data between multiple systems, devices, and partners, making it vulnerable to cyberattacks, data breaches, and system failures. Protecting sensitive information, such as customer data, financial records, and proprietary business information, is crucial for businesses adopting Logistics 4.0 technologies.

Data Privacy and Security: With the increased use of IoT devices, sensors, and cloud-based platforms, supply chains generate massive amounts of data. Protecting this data from unauthorized access, hacking, or theft is a top priority. A single data breach can have severe financial and reputational consequences for a company.

Vulnerabilities in IoT Devices: IoT devices are essential for real-time tracking and monitoring in Logistics 4.0, but they can also be a weak point in the supply chain's cybersecurity defense. IoT devices are often targeted by hackers due to their connectivity and lack of robust security features. Securing IoT networks and devices is critical to preventing cyber threats.

Blockchain and Cryptography Risks: While blockchain is often praised for its security features, businesses must still ensure that the cryptographic keys used to secure blockchain transactions are properly managed. Poor key management or vulnerabilities in the blockchain network could compromise the integrity of the entire supply chain.

To mitigate these risks, companies must implement robust cybersecurity measures across their supply chains. This includes encrypting data, securing IoT devices with strong authentication protocols, regularly updating software and firmware, and conducting regular cybersecurity audits. Additionally, businesses should educate their employees on cybersecurity best practices and establish protocols for responding to potential threats.

Resistance to Change and Workforce Adaptation

One of the most significant challenges in adopting Logistics 4.0 is overcoming resistance to change within the organization. Employees, especially those who have worked with traditional supply chain processes for many years, may be hesitant to adopt new technologies or fear that automation could replace their jobs.

Workforce Displacement: Automation technologies such as robotics and AI can reduce the need for manual labor in certain areas of the supply chain. This has led to concerns about workforce displacement, where employees fear losing their jobs to machines. Addressing these concerns and ensuring that workers feel secure in their roles is essential for a smooth transition.

Skill Gaps: Logistics 4.0 requires a workforce with specialized skills in data analytics, machine learning, AI, and automation systems. Many businesses face challenges in finding and retaining employees with the expertise needed to operate these advanced technologies. Upskilling the current workforce is essential, but it can also be time-consuming and costly.

Cultural Resistance: Organizational culture plays a significant role in the adoption of new technologies. If a company's leadership and employees are not aligned with the digital transformation goals, they may resist change. Overcoming cultural resistance requires strong leadership, clear communication, and a commitment to fostering a culture of innovation.

To address these challenges, companies should focus on changing management strategies that engage employees in the digital transformation process. Providing training programs, fostering a culture of innovation, and involving employees in decision-making can help ease the transition and reduce resistance to change. Moreover, businesses should emphasize that Logistics 4.0 is not about replacing workers but empowering them with the tools they need to be more efficient and productive.

Lack of Standardization and Interoperability

As companies adopt various Logistics 4.0 technologies, a lack of standardization and interoperability across platforms can create challenges in implementing an integrated, seamless supply chain. Different systems and devices may use different data formats, protocols, or standards, making it difficult for them to communicate effectively with each other.

Fragmented Technology Ecosystems: Many companies adopt solutions from multiple vendors, each with their own proprietary technology. Without standardization, these fragmented ecosystems can create compatibility issues and limit the full potential of Logistics 4.0.

Supply Chain Collaboration: Logistics 4.0 often involves collaboration between multiple stakeholders, including suppliers, manufacturers, distributors, and logistics providers. Ensuring that all parties use compatible systems and standards is essential for smooth collaboration and data sharing.

To overcome these challenges, industry-wide standards for Logistics 4.0 technologies and data formats need to be established. Initiatives like the Open Logistics Foundation and other industry consortia are working toward creating common standards that ensure interoperability between different platforms and systems. Businesses should also prioritize choosing technologies that support open standards and are easily integrable with other systems.

Navigating Regulatory Compliance and Legal Challenges

Adopting Logistics 4.0 technologies can also create challenges in navigating regulatory compliance and addressing legal concerns, particularly in highly regulated industries such as pharmaceuticals, food, and chemicals.

The use of blockchain, AI, and data analytics in supply chains introduces new legal and regulatory considerations that businesses must be prepared to address.

Data Privacy Laws: The collection and sharing of data in Logistics 4.0 must comply with global data privacy regulations such as the General Data Protection Regulation (GDPR) in Europe or the California Consumer Privacy Act (CCPA) in the United States. Ensuring that sensitive data is collected, stored, and shared in a compliant manner is crucial for businesses to avoid legal penalties.

Cross-Border Regulations: Global supply chains often involve multiple countries with different regulatory requirements. Navigating these cross-border regulations, especially when it comes to data sharing and transportation, can be complex. Ensuring compliance with international trade laws and industry-specific regulations is essential for maintaining a seamless supply chain.

Liability and Accountability: The use of automation and AI introduces questions of liability in the event of errors or failures. For example, if an autonomous delivery vehicle is involved in an accident or if an AI system makes a flawed decision that disrupts the supply chain, determining liability can be challenging. Businesses must establish clear legal frameworks to address these issues.

To manage these challenges, companies should work closely with legal experts and regulatory bodies to ensure compliance with all relevant laws. Additionally, businesses must establish clear policies for data governance, liability, and accountability to address potential legal concerns related to Logistics 4.0 technologies.

Overcoming the Challenges of Logistics 4.0

While the challenges of adopting Logistics 4.0 are significant, they are not insurmountable. By taking a strategic approach to digital transformation, businesses can overcome these obstacles and fully realize the benefits of Logistics 4.0. Key steps include:

Investing in Integration Solutions: Companies should prioritize investments in integration tools and technologies that allow legacy systems to communicate with modern platforms. This ensures a smooth transition and minimizes operational disruption.

Building Cybersecurity Resilience: Strong cybersecurity protocols are essential for protecting data and ensuring the security of Logistics 4.0 systems. Businesses must invest in robust security measures, regularly update software, and train employees in cybersecurity best practices.

Fostering a Culture of Innovation: Successful adoption of Logistics 4.0 requires a workforce that embraces change and is open to innovation. Companies should focus on creating a culture that encourages experimentation, rewards innovation, and empowers employees with the skills they need to succeed in a digital supply chain.

Partnering with Industry Leaders: Collaborating with technology providers, industry associations, and other businesses can help companies stay informed about the latest developments in Logistics 4.0 and ensure they are adopting the best practices.

The Road Ahead for Logistics 4.0

The adoption of Logistics 4.0 technologies is a transformative journey that promises to revolutionize supply chain management. While businesses face challenges in terms of cost, integration, cybersecurity, and workforce adaptation, the potential rewards far outweigh the risks. By addressing these challenges strategically, companies can create smarter, more resilient, and more efficient supply chains that are capable of thriving in the digital age.

CHAPTER TEN
The Future of Supply Chain Management

As we move into the next era of global commerce, supply chains are set to undergo profound transformations, driven by the rapid advancement of technology, changing consumer expectations, and the increasing need for sustainability. Logistics 4.0 represents a significant step forward, but the future of supply chain management extends beyond the technologies we've explored thus far. In this chapter, we'll examine the emerging trends, innovations, and strategies that will shape the future of supply chain management and how businesses can prepare for this next wave of evolution.

Autonomous Supply Chains

The concept of an autonomous supply chain—a fully automated, self-regulating system that requires minimal human intervention—is quickly becoming a reality. Advances in artificial intelligence (AI), machine learning, and robotics are enabling supply chains to operate with greater autonomy, from production and warehousing to transportation and delivery.

Autonomous Vehicles and Drones: Autonomous trucks, ships, and drones are revolutionizing transportation and last-mile delivery. These vehicles, equipped with AI and sensor technologies, can optimize routes, reduce fuel consumption, and deliver goods without the need for human drivers. In urban areas, drones are being used to bypass traffic and deliver packages directly to consumers' doorsteps, reducing delivery times and emissions.

Automated Warehousing: Smart warehouses powered by robotics and AI are becoming more autonomous, handling tasks such as picking, packing, and sorting with minimal human involvement. As automation technologies continue to advance, we can expect to see fully autonomous warehouses where robots and AI systems manage inventory, process orders, and maintain equipment.

Self-Learning Systems: AI and machine learning algorithms are increasingly being used to create self-learning supply chains. These systems continuously learn from data, adjusting operations in real-time to optimize performance. For example, AI can predict demand fluctuations, optimize production schedules, and adjust transportation routes based on real-time conditions.

While the transition to autonomous supply chains offers significant benefits—such as reduced labor costs, faster processing times, and improved efficiency, it also presents challenges. Companies must invest in the necessary infrastructure, address cybersecurity concerns, and ensure that their workforce is prepared to manage and maintain autonomous systems.

Hyper-Personalization and the Customer-Centric Supply Chain

As consumer expectations continue to evolve, the demand for hyper-personalization is reshaping the supply chain. In the future, supply chains will need to become more flexible, agile, and customer-centric, allowing businesses to deliver personalized products and services on a scale.

On-Demand Manufacturing: With the rise of technologies such as 3D printing and advanced manufacturing, businesses can produce customized products on-demand, reducing the need for large inventories and enabling faster delivery times. For example, a fashion brand could use 3D printing to create personalized clothing items based on individual customer preferences, delivering them within days rather than weeks.

Customizable Delivery Options: Consumers increasingly expect personalized delivery experiences, including the ability to choose delivery windows, locations, and methods. AI and data analytics will play a key role in optimizing these delivery options, allowing businesses to offer customers greater flexibility without compromising efficiency.

Customer Data Integration: The future supply chain will be closely integrated with customer data, enabling businesses to anticipate consumer needs and adjust operations accordingly. By analyzing customer purchasing behavior, preferences, and feedback, supply chains can become more responsive to individual demands, enhancing customer satisfaction and loyalty.

Hyper-personalization will require businesses to adopt more agile and flexible supply chain models that can quickly adapt to changing consumer preferences. Companies that succeed in creating customer-centric supply chains will have a significant competitive advantage in the future marketplace.

Circular Economy and Closed-Loop Supply Chains

The transition to a circular economy, where products and materials are reused, refurbished, and recycled, is becoming increasingly important as businesses seek to reduce waste, conserve resources, and promote sustainability. In a circular economy, supply chains shift from linear models—where products are manufactured, used, and discarded—to closed-loop systems that prioritize reuse and resource efficiency.

Product Lifecycle Management: In a closed-loop supply chain, businesses focus on extending the lifecycle of products through repair, refurbishment, and recycling. For example, a technology company may design products that can be easily disassembled and upgraded, allowing consumers to replace components rather than buying new devices.

Reverse Logistics: Managing the flow of returned products is a critical component of circular supply chains. Businesses must develop efficient reverse logistics processes that allow them to recover products, assess their condition, and determine whether they can be repaired, refurbished, or recycled. Technologies like blockchain and IoT play a key role in tracking products throughout their lifecycle and ensuring transparency in the reverse logistics process.

Waste Reduction and Resource Efficiency: By adopting circular supply chain practices, businesses can reduce waste and optimize resource use. For example, manufacturers can use data analytics and AI to minimize material waste during production, while recycling technologies can recover valuable materials from end-of-life products.

The shift toward circular supply chains is not only driven by environmental concerns but also by the potential for cost savings and new revenue streams. Companies that embrace the circular economy will be well-positioned to meet sustainability goals and reduce their environmental footprint.

Supply Chain Resilience and Risk Management

The COVID-19 pandemic, natural disasters, and geopolitical tensions have exposed vulnerabilities in global supply chains, highlighting the need for greater supply chain resilience. In the future, businesses will prioritize building resilient supply chains that can withstand disruptions and recover quickly from unexpected events.

Diversification of Suppliers: To reduce the risk of supply chain disruptions, businesses will move away from relying on a single supplier or region for critical materials. Instead, companies will diversify their supplier base, creating a more resilient supply chain that can adapt to disruptions in specific regions or markets.

Supply Chain Visibility: Real-time visibility into supply chain operations will be essential for managing risk. Technologies like IoT, blockchain, and AI will enable businesses to monitor the movement of goods, track inventory levels, and identify potential disruptions in real-time, allowing them to respond quickly and minimize impact.

Scenario Planning and Predictive Analytics: AI-powered predictive analytics will play a key role in anticipating potential risks and disruptions. By analyzing data on weather patterns, geopolitical events, and market trends, businesses can simulate different scenarios and develop contingency plans to mitigate risks.

The future supply chain will need to be both agile and resilient, capable of adapting to changing conditions while maintaining continuity in operations. Companies that invest in building resilience will be better prepared to navigate the uncertainties of the global economy.

Advanced Robotics and Automation

Automation will continue to play a pivotal role in the future of supply chain management. As robotic technologies become more sophisticated, they will take on increasingly complex tasks, further enhancing efficiency and productivity in warehouses, factories, and distribution centers.

Collaborative Robots (Cobots): Cobots, designed to work alongside human workers, will play a key role in automating tasks that require precision and flexibility. Unlike traditional industrial robots, cobots are equipped with advanced sensors and AI, allowing them to collaborate with humans in a safe and efficient manner. For example, cobots can assist in tasks such as picking, packing, and sorting in warehouses, improving productivity while reducing labor costs.

AI-Powered Robotics: The integration of AI with robotics will enable machines to perform more complex tasks autonomously. AI-powered robots will be able to learn from data, make decisions in real-time, and adapt to changing conditions, allowing them to handle tasks such as quality control, inventory management, and equipment maintenance with minimal human intervention.

Automation in Manufacturing and Distribution: Automation will play a central role in future manufacturing and distribution operations. Factories of the future will be highly automated, with robots handling tasks such as assembling products, transporting materials, and inspecting quality. Distribution centers will become fully automated, with robots managing the flow of goods from storage to shipping.

While automation offers significant benefits in terms of efficiency and cost savings, businesses must also address challenges related to workforce adaptation, system integration, and cybersecurity. The future of supply chain management will require a careful balance between human workers and advanced robotics to achieve optimal outcomes.

AI and Machine Learning for Supply Chain Optimization

AI and machine learning will continue to drive innovation in supply chain management, enabling businesses to make smarter, data-driven decisions and optimize every aspect of their operations.

Predictive Analytics for Demand Forecasting: AI-powered predictive analytics will enable businesses to forecast demand with greater accuracy, helping them optimize inventory levels, production schedules, and transportation routes. By analyzing data from multiple sources—such as sales trends, weather patterns, and social media, AI can predict fluctuations in demand and adjust operations accordingly.

Dynamic Pricing and Inventory Management: AI algorithms can also be used to optimize pricing and inventory management in real-time. For example, a retailer could use AI to adjust product prices based on factors such as demand, competition, and inventory levels, maximizing profitability while minimizing the risk of stockouts or overstocking.

Supply Chain Automation and Decision-Making: As AI systems become more advanced, they will take on greater responsibility for automating supply chain decisions. AI algorithms will be able to analyze large volumes of data, identify trends, and make real-time decisions on everything from production and procurement to transportation and distribution.

The future of supply chain management will be defined by intelligent systems that can optimize operations, predict outcomes, and adapt to changing conditions with minimal human intervention. Businesses that invest in AI and machine learning will be able to streamline their supply chains, reduce costs, and improve service levels.

Preparing for the Future of Supply Chain Management

As we look ahead, it's clear that supply chain management will continue to evolve rapidly. The integration of advanced technologies such as AI, robotics, IoT, and blockchain will enable businesses to create smarter, more efficient, and more sustainable supply chains. However, realizing the full potential of these technologies requires careful planning, investment, and a willingness to adapt to new ways of working.

To prepare for the future of supply chain management, businesses should:

Invest in Technology: Companies must continue to invest in the technologies that will drive the future of supply chains, including AI, automation, and IoT. These investments will provide the foundation for creating more efficient and resilient operations.

Build a Skilled Workforce: As supply chains become more automated and data-driven, businesses will need a workforce with the skills to manage and operate advanced technologies. Upskilling employees and attracting talent with expertise in AI, robotics, and data analytics will be critical for success.

Embrace Sustainability: Sustainability will play a central role in the future of supply chain management. Businesses must adopt circular economic practices, reduce their environmental impact, and meet the growing demand for sustainable products and services.

Foster Agility and Resilience: The supply chains of the future must be agile and resilient, capable of adapting to changing conditions and recovering from disruptions. Businesses should focus on building flexibility into their supply chains, diversifying suppliers, and using data to anticipate risks.

Conclusion: A New Era for Supply Chains

The future of supply chain management is full of opportunities and challenges. The technologies that define Logistics 4.0 are just the beginning of a larger transformation that will reshape how goods are produced, moved, and delivered across the globe. Businesses that embrace this transformation, invest in innovation, and prioritize sustainability will be well-positioned to thrive in the rapidly changing global marketplace. The road ahead is full of possibilities, and the time to act is now. By adopting the principles and technologies of Logistics 4.0, companies can create supply chains that are not only more efficient and cost-effective but also more sustainable, resilient, and responsive to the needs of tomorrow's consumers.

Appendix

Key Terms and Definitions

This section provides a glossary of key terms and concepts used throughout the book to help readers better understand the terminology of Logistics 4.0.

Artificial Intelligence (AI): The simulation of human intelligence by machines, particularly computer systems, enabling tasks such as learning, reasoning, and problem-solving.

Blockchain: A decentralized digital ledger that records transactions across multiple computers, ensuring security, transparency, and immutability.

Internet of Things (IoT): A network of physical objects embedded with sensors, software, and other technologies to connect and exchange data with other devices and systems over the internet.

Predictive Analytics: Techniques that use historical data, machine learning, and statistical algorithms to forecast future outcomes.

Supply Chain: The entire process of producing and delivering goods or services, from raw materials to the end customer.

Automation: The use of technology to perform tasks with minimal human intervention, improving efficiency and reducing errors.

Tools and Technologies for Logistics 4.0

Here are some of the most commonly used tools and technologies mentioned throughout the book, along with their applications in supply chain management:

Warehouse Management Systems (WMS): Software applications that manage and optimize warehouse operations, including inventory tracking, order fulfillment, and shipping.

Transport Management Systems (TMS): A system designed to plan, execute, and optimize the movement of goods, ensuring efficient and cost-effective transportation.

Collaborative Robots (Cobots): Robots designed to work alongside human workers in warehouses and factories, assisting in tasks such as picking and packing.

Blockchain Platforms: Distributed ledger technology solutions, such as Hyperledger or Ethereum, used to track goods, verify transactions, and ensure transparency in supply chains.

AI Analytics Tools: Software such as IBM Watson or Google Cloud AI that analyzes supply chain data to forecast demand, optimize operations, and improve decision-making.

Case Studies and Real-World Examples

This section provides a summary of notable case studies referenced in the book, showcasing how various companies have successfully implemented Logistics 4.0 technologies.

Walmart's Blockchain for Food Traceability: Walmart implemented blockchain technology to enhance traceability in its food supply chain, reducing the time it takes to trace the origin of products from days to seconds.

Amazon's Robotics in Warehousing: Amazon's use of robotics in its fulfillment centers has drastically improved efficiency, allowing the company to handle millions of orders during peak seasons with minimal errors.

Unilever's Circular Supply Chain: Unilever has implemented sustainable supply chain practices, focusing on circular economy principles by reducing plastic waste and promoting recycling through blockchain technology.

Resources for Further Learning

For readers who wish to explore the topics discussed in the book more deeply, the following resources are recommended:

Books:

Supply Chain Revolution by Suman Sarkar

The Fourth Industrial Revolution by Klaus Schwab

The AI Advantage: How to Put the Artificial Intelligence Revolution to Work by Thomas H. Davenport

Online Courses:

MITx Micro master's in supply chain management: A comprehensive online program covering supply chain design, technology, and analytics.

Coursera's AI for Everyone by Andrew Ng: A beginner-friendly course on the basics of artificial intelligence and its applications in various industries.

Industry Reports:

Gartner's Supply Chain Technology Trends Report: A yearly report highlighting the latest trends and innovations in supply chain technology.

McKinsey & Company's Report on Digital Supply Chains: Insights into the digital transformation of global supply chains and the role of new technologies.

Common Challenges and Solutions in Logistics 4.0

This section offers a quick reference to common challenges businesses may face when implementing Logistics 4.0 technologies, along with suggested solutions:

Challenge: High initial cost of adopting new technologies.

Solution: Start with small-scale implementations, focusing on technologies that offer quick ROI, such as warehouse automation or predictive analytics.

Challenge: Integrating new technologies with legacy systems.

Solution: Use APIs and middleware to bridge the gap between legacy systems and modern technologies, ensuring smooth data flow and communication.

Challenge: Cybersecurity risks due to increased digital connectivity.

Solution: Implement robust cybersecurity measures, including encryption, firewalls, regular software updates, and employee training on security best practices.

Sample Templates for Supply Chain Optimization

To help readers apply the principles discussed in the book, this section includes sample templates for supply chain optimization:

Inventory Optimization Template: A simple spreadsheet template for tracking inventory levels, lead times, and reorder points to ensure optimal stock levels and minimize carrying costs.

Supplier Performance Evaluation Template: A tool for assessing the performance of suppliers based on metrics such as on-time delivery, quality, and pricing.

Risk Assessment Matrix: A template for identifying potential risks in the supply chain and assigning risk levels based on likelihood and impact, helping businesses prioritize mitigation efforts.

Industry Standards and Certifications

For businesses looking to meet industry standards and stay competitive, this section outlines key certifications and standards related to supply chain management and Logistics 4.0:

ISO 9001: A quality management standard that ensures products and services meet customer expectations and regulatory requirements.

ISO 28000: A security management system for the supply chain, focusing on reducing risks related to logistics operations.

APICS Certified Supply Chain Professional (CSCP): A globally recognized certification that covers supply chain management, logistics, and operations.

Glossary of Acronyms

A list of acronyms used throughout the book for quick reference:

- AI: Artificial Intelligence

- IoT: Internet of Things

- WMS: Warehouse Management System

- TMS: Transportation Management System

- ASRS: Automated Storage and Retrieval System

- ERP: Enterprise Resource Planning

About The Author

Clive Akhalumenyo is a highly regarded supply chain expert, known for his transformative impact on logistics and operations management. With a career defined by a relentless pursuit of efficiency and innovation, he has established himself as a leading authority in the field. His strategic insights and forward-thinking solutions have not only earned him widespread recognition but also revolutionized how businesses optimize their supply chains. Specializing in the integration of advanced technologies such as artificial intelligence, blockchain, and automation, He has been instrumental in enhancing transparency, efficiency, and sustainability across global supply chains. His work is characterized by a commitment to leveraging data-driven approaches to solve complex supply chain challenges and create agile, resilient operations.

A champion of collaboration, He has forged strong partnerships within the industry, driving progress and setting new standards for excellence. His passion for mentoring the next generation of supply chain professionals is evident in his dedication to sharing knowledge and fostering talent. He is also a strong advocate for sustainability, continuously seeking ways to promote environmentally responsible practices in supply chain management. Renowned as a thought leader and visionary, Clive Akhalumenyo is a sought-after speaker at industry conferences and forums, where he continues to inspire innovation and guide the future of supply chain management. His expertise, combined with a deep commitment to advancing the field, makes him a key voice in shaping the future of logistics and operations.

www.ingramcontent.com/pod-product-compliance
Lightning Source LLC
LaVergne TN
LVHW042243070526
838201LV00088B/4